50 Delicious Slow Cooker Chili Recipes

(50 Delicious Slow Cooker Chili Recipes - Volume 1)

Carol Miller

Copyright: Published in the United States by Carol Miller/ © CAROL MILLER

Published on November, 24 2020

All rights reserved. No part of this publication may be reproduced, stored in retrieval system, copied in any form or by any means, electronic, mechanical, photocopying, recording or otherwise transmitted without written permission from the publisher. Please do not participate in or encourage piracy of this material in any way. You must not circulate this book in any format. CAROL MILLER does not control or direct users' actions and is not responsible for the information or content shared, harm and/or actions of the book readers.

In accordance with the U.S. Copyright Act of 1976, the scanning, uploading and electronic sharing of any part of this book without the permission of the publisher constitute unlawful piracy and theft of the author's intellectual property. If you would like to use material from the book (other than just simply for reviewing the book), prior permission must be obtained by contacting the author at author@limerecipes.com

Thank you for your support of the author's rights.

Content

50 AWESOME SLOW COOKER CHILI RECIPES 4

1. Bacon And Mushroom Chili Recipe 4
2. Brown Sugar Chili Recipe 4
3. Chili Cheese Dip Crock Pot Recipe 4
4. Chili Recipe 5
5. Chipotle Chili Recipe 5
6. Cincinnati Chili Heads South Recipe 6
7. Comforting Crockpot Chili Recipe 6
8. Crock Pot Chili Slow Burn Chili Recipe 7
9. Crock Pot Chili Recipe 7
10. Crock Pot Pork Chili Verde Recipe 7
11. Crock Pot White Chili Recipe 8
12. Crock Pot White Chicken Chili With Hominy Recipe 8
13. Crock Pot Chili Recipe 9
14. Crockpot Beef Chili Recipe 9
15. Crockpot Chili Beans Recipe 9
16. Crockpot Chili Recipe 10
17. Crockpot Chili Soup Recipe 10
18. Crockpot White Bean Chicken Chili Recipe 11
19. Crockpot White Chicken Chipolte Chili Recipe 11
20. Dads Crockpot Chili No Tomato Recipe . 11
21. Easy Chilli Recipe 12
22. Easy Crock Pot Chili Cheese Dip Recipe . 12
23. Fire Nation Chili Recipe 12
24. Homemade Beef Chili In The Crockpot Recipe 13
25. Homemade Pork Chili In The Crock Pot Recipe 13
26. Jimmy Fallons Crock Pot Chili Recipe 13
27. Kate's Google Chili Recipe 14
28. My Chili Ctme Recipe 15
29. My Chili Valentine Recipe 16
30. New And Improved Crock Pot Pork Chili Verde Recipe 16
31. Rustic Chili Recipe 17
32. Slo Cooker Chili Recipe 17
33. Slow Cooker Beef Chili Recipe 18
34. Slow Cooker Chicken Chili Recipe 18
35. Slow Cooker Chili Beef Stew Recipe 19
36. Slow Cooker Chili Recipe 19
37. Slow Cooker Mexican Pork Chili Recipe .. 19
38. Slow Cooker Pork Butt Green Chili Recipe 20
39. Slow Cooker Pumpkin Chili Recipe 20
40. Slow Cooker White Bean And Chicken Chili Recipe 21
41. Slow Cooker Black Bean Chili Recipe 21
42. Slow Cooker Chili Recipe 22
43. Spicy Pork Green Chili Crock Pot Recipe 23
44. Stupid Easy Crock Pot Chili Recipe 23
45. Tailgate Slow Cooker Chili Recipe 23
46. Turkey Chili For The Crock Pot Recipe ... 24
47. Vegan Slow Cooker Chili Recipe 24
48. Vegetarian Crockpot Chili Recipe 25
49. Vegetarian Crock Pot Chili Recipe 25
50. Very Old Meatloaf Recipe 25

INDEX 27
CONCLUSION 28

50 Awesome Slow Cooker Chili Recipes

***

1. Bacon And Mushroom Chili Recipe

Serving: 8 | Prep: | Cook: 4hours3mins | Ready in:

Ingredients

- 1/2 pkg bacon, chopped
- 1/2 small onion diced
- 1 container mushrooms, quartered or sliced
- salt & pepper
- 1 can rotel tomatoes
- 4 cups chicken broth
- 2 chicken bouillon cubes
- 2 tbsp brown sugar
- 1 tbsp Dijon mustard
- 1 tsp prepared horseradish
- 1 1/2 tsp parsley
- 1 tsp cilantro
- 1-2 tsp chili powder, to taste
- 2 cans black beans, drained and rinsed
- 1 can kidney beans, drained and rinsed
- 1 can chili beans in sauce, undrained

Direction

- In a large pot or Dutch oven, fry bacon over medium to medium high heat. When bacon is almost crispy, reserving 2 Tbsp. in the pan, drain rest of fat.
- Add onions and mushrooms, salt and pepper to taste (a generous pinch of each is about right) then sauté until onions are soft.
- Add tomatoes, broth, and next 7 ingredients. Bring to a boil, turn heat down and let simmer 15 minutes. (If using a crockpot, turn heat off, leaving pot on burner, then proceed to next step)
- Add chili beans and sauce, drained kidney and black beans, and simmer at least 30 mins. (Crockpot method: spray inside of crockpot with pan spray, omit simmer time, transfer to crockpot on low setting for 3-4 hours)

2. Brown Sugar Chili Recipe

Serving: 6 | Prep: | Cook: 2hours | Ready in:

Ingredients

- 1lb. extra lean ground beef
- 1/2c brown sugar
- 2Tbsp mustard
- 1 medium onion, chopped
- 2 cans kidney beans, drained
- 1 pint tomato juice
- 1/2tsp salt
- 1/4tsp pepper
- 1tsp chili powder

Direction

- Brown ground beef & onion.
- Stir in sugar and mustard.
- Combine all ingredients in slow cooker.
- Cook on high 2 hr., stirring 3 times.

3. Chili Cheese Dip Crock Pot Recipe

Serving: 4 | Prep: | Cook: 16mins | Ready in:

Ingredients

- 1 (11 oz.) can condensed chili beef soup
- 3 oz. pkg. cream cheese, softened
- 1/2 cup sour cream

- 1 Tablespoon water
- 1 teaspoon prepared mustard
- 1 teaspoon worcestershire sauce
- 1 teaspoon chili sauce (add to taste)
- 1 teaspoon hot pepper sauce, optional (add to taste)

Direction

- In slow cooker/Crock Pot, combine all ingredients; mix well.
- Cover and cook on LOW for 1 1/2 to 2 hours, stirring occasionally, or until cheese is melted and dip is hot.
- Serve warm with tortilla or corn chips.
- Makes 2 cups.

4. Chili Recipe

Serving: 5 | Prep: | Cook: 2hours | Ready in:

Ingredients

- 2 pounds lean ground beef
- 1 (46 fluid ounce) Can tomato juice
- 1 (29 ounce) can tomato sauce
- 1 (15 ounce) can kidney beans, drained and rinsed
- 1 (15 ounce) can pinto beans, drained and rinsed
- 1 ½ cups Chopped onion
- ¼ cup Chopped green bell pepper
- ⅛ tsp ground cayenne pepper
- ½ tsp White sugar
- ½ tsp Dried oregano
- ½ tsp ground black pepper
- 1 tsp salt
- 1 ½ tsp ground cumin
- ¼ cup chili powder

Direction

- Place ground beef in a large, deep skillet. Cook over medium-high heat until evenly brown. Drain, and crumble.
- In a large pot over high heat combine the ground beef, tomato juice, tomato sauce, kidney beans, pinto beans, onions, bell pepper, cayenne pepper, sugar, oregano, ground black pepper, salt, cumin and chili powder. Bring to a boil, then reduce heat to low.
- Simmer for 1 ½ hours.
- If using a slow cooker, set on low, add ingredients, and cook for 8 to 10 hours.

5. Chipotle Chili Recipe

Serving: 12 | Prep: | Cook: 2hours | Ready in:

Ingredients

- 2 lbs ground beef
- 1 lb italian sausage
- 1 large onion, diced
- 1 Tbsp garlic, minced
- 2 ribs celery, coarsely chopped
- 1 green pepper, coarsely chopped
- 1/2 red pepper, coarsely chopped
- 2 14.5 oz cans crushed tomatoes
- 2 14.5 oz cans diced tomatoes
- 2 16 oz cans kidney beans, drained
- 2 16oz cans chili beans in medium or hot sauce
- 1/2 7.5oz can chipotle peppers in adobo sauce (or more to taste), chopped
- 1/2 3oz bag Real bacon bits
- 2 Tbsp chili sauce
- 2 tsp cup Frank's red hot sauce
- 1 Tbsp chili powder
- 1/4 tsp cumin
- 1/4 tsp salt
- 2 tsp brown sugar

Direction

- In a large pan, combine ground beef and sausage and brown. When about half browned, add in onion and garlic.
- Add beef mixture and rest of the ingredients to a slow cooker.

- Cover and cook on low until veggies are completely done. I like my peppers completely done, but the celery to have just the slightest bite left to them. (6 to 8 hours on low - 3 to 4 hours on high)

6. Cincinnati Chili Heads South Recipe

Serving: 6 | Prep: | Cook: 4hours3mins | Ready in:

Ingredients

- For Chili
- 2lb ground meat(beef, venison, lamb, pork, chicken, turkey, all can prolly be used....I used venison, as I do with our chili)
- 1 large onion chopped
- 3 cloves garlic, minced
- 1 1/2 cup beef stock
- 28ish oz tomato sauce
- 1T red wine vinegar
- 1T worcestershire sauce
- 1 clove garlic, minced
- 3T chili powder
- 1-2t cinnamon
- 3t cumin
- 1t celery powder
- 1T quality paprika(I used smoked)
- 1/2-1t red pepper flakes
- 1/2t cayenne(it was tough to not use more, but this is only meant to have a very slight heat..so use your judgment)
- 1T cocoa
- kosher or sea salt and fresh ground black pepper
- For Serving
- 1lb spaghetti
- 1 large can chili beans
- 8oz colby or cheddar cheese, shredded
- green or red onions, onions

Direction

- Put all chili ingredients in slow cooker (a small one works well) and cook on low for about 3 hours.
- Stir and remove lid and cook another hour, if necessary, to thicken.
- To Serve
- Cook spaghetti per package directions and drain
- Heat chili beans through
- Top a serving of spaghetti with a large spoonful of the chili mixture, then top with small spoonful of beans.
- Add shredded cheese and chopped onions

7. Comforting Crockpot Chili Recipe

Serving: 8 | Prep: | Cook: 4mins | Ready in:

Ingredients

- 1 pound ground turkey breast or very lean ground beef
- 1 large onion - finely chopped
- 5 oz pinto beans - rinsed and drained
- 8.5 oz corn rinsed and drained
- 15 oz tomato sauce
- 14.5 oz diced tomatoes
- 10 oz diced tomato and green chilies
- 1 tbsp chili powder
- 1 tsp ground cumin
- 1/2 tsp garlic powder
- 1/2 tsp salt

Direction

- Cook beef in nonstick skillet over medium heat until no longer pink.
- Transfer meat to crockpot, add remaining ingredients and stir until combined. Cook on high for 4 hours.
- 8 servings, one cup per serving

8. Crock Pot Chili Slow Burn Chili Recipe

Serving: 0 | Prep: | Cook: 8hours6mins | Ready in:

Ingredients

- 1 red bell pepper (diced)
- 2 Jalepenos (minced)
- 5 Pablano peppers(roasted in oven)
- 1 anaheim chili (roasted in oven)are also called California chili or Magdalena
- 2 sweet onions Vidallia (diced)
- 1 Head of garlic (pureed/crushed/minced)
- 1lb Angus steak
- 1 Link turkey smoked sausage (12inches)
- 1lb ground beef Chuck
- 1lb mild Italian sausage
- 1 lb hot Italian sausage Links
- 1 Teaspoon onion powder
- 1 Teaspoon garlic powder
- 3 Tablespoon chili powder
- 1 Teaspoon paprika
- 1 1/2 Teaspoon ground cumin
- 1 Teaspoon coriander
- 1/2 Teaspoon ground red pepper
- salt and pepper to taste
- 2 Cup tomato sauce(Ragu roasted garlic and onion)
- 1 Cup tomato paste
- 1 12oz Light beer
- 1 Cup chicken stock
- 2 15oz canned kidney beans
- 2 15oz canned pinto beans
- 2 tablespoon unsalted butter
- 3 Tablespoon olive oil

Direction

- Brown all meats separately. Dice your steak up into little cubes then on high heat sear the outside salting and peppering your meat as it cooks. You don't want to cook it all the way.
- As you cook the meats set them aside in a strainer. Slice up the cooked sausage once cooled. In same pan used to cook the steak add your Onions, Jalapeños, Red Bell Pepper, unsalted butter and olive oil. On med heat cook till soft then add your garlic cook for 1 min.
- In a separate large pot start the heat on Low. Add your meats and mix. Then add the contents of the steak pan to the meat mix. Once mixed add your Onion Powder, Garlic Powder, Coriander, Cumin, Red Pepper, Chili powder, and Paprika; Stir.
- Now add your tomato sauce and paste; Stir. Slowly add your chicken broth and beer. Move heat up to bring to a simmer. Add salt and pepper about 1 tablespoon salt and 1/2 tablespoon Black pepper. Simmer on low heat for about 30 min before transferring to crock pot. Cook on low for 4-8 hrs.

9. Crock Pot Chili Recipe

Serving: 10 | Prep: | Cook: 120mins | Ready in:

Ingredients

- 2 (8 oz.) cans tomato sauce
- 2 (16 oz.) cans dark red kidney beans, undrained
- 1 lb. hamburger meat
- 3 or 4 tbsp. chili powder

Direction

- 1. Cook the hamburger meat and drain well.
- 2. Mix all ingredients together in crock pot.
- 3. Cook on high for at least 1 to 2 hours. Stir occasionally.

10. Crock Pot Pork Chili Verde Recipe

Serving: 10 | Prep: | Cook: 420mins | Ready in:

Ingredients

- 3 lbs pork shoulder
- 28 oz can of green chili enchilada sauce
- 7 oz can of diced green chili's
- 1 tsp cumin
- pinch of salt
- pinch of pepper
- 2 chopped cloves of garlic
- 1 medium onion
- 1/2 bottle of mexican beer(i use Pacifico)
- 1 cup sour cream
- extras:
- tortillas
- sour cream
- cheese

Direction

- Chop the garlic and dice and brown the onion in a skillet with a little oil. Put into crock pot.
- Cut the pork into cubes. Add to skillet and cook until just brown on sides. Put into crock pot.
- Deglaze pan with beer and pour into crock pot.
- Pour green enchilada sauce, green chilies, cumin, salt and pepper into crock pot.
- Give it a good stir.
- Cook on High for 1 hour.
- Switch to Low and cook for another 7 hours.
- (Crock pot liner works great)
- Stir in 1 cup sour cream at the end of cooking before serving.
- Serve with refried beans and rice. Makes excellent burritos!

11. Crock Pot White Chili Recipe

Serving: 6 | Prep: | Cook: 3mins | Ready in:

Ingredients

- 4 chicken breast cut into bitesize pieces
- 1 pound of dry great northern beans (soaked overnight in water then drained)
- 8 oz can chopped green chilies
- 1 onion (chopped)
- garlic (chopped; to taste)
- 2 tsp cumming
- 1 tsp oregano
- 1 1/2 tsp cayanne pepper
- 1/2 tsp salt
- 1 cup water
- 14.5 oz chicken broth

Direction

- Place all into crock pot and cook on low for 10 to 12 hours.

12. Crock Pot White Chicken Chili With Hominy Recipe

Serving: 6 | Prep: | Cook: 5mins | Ready in:

Ingredients

- 1 1/4 pounds boneless skinless chicken thighs
- 2 cans (15.8 ounces each) great northern beans, rinsed and drained
- 1 can (15.5 ounces) white hominy, drained
- 1 envelope (1.25 ounces) Old El Paso® taco seasoning mix
- 1 can (4.5 ounces) Old El Paso® chopped green chiles
- 1 can (10 3/4 ounces) condensed reduced-sodium cream of mushroom soup
- sour cream, if desired
- Chopped green onions, if desired

Direction

- Place chicken in 3- to 4-quart slow cooker.
- Top with remaining ingredients except sour cream and onions.
- Cover and cook on low heat setting 8 to 10 hours.
- Before serving, stir gently to break up chicken pieces.
- Serve topped with sour cream and onions.
- *************************************

- Note: I omit the green chilies because I like it milder.

13. Crock Pot Chili Recipe

Serving: 12 | Prep: | Cook: 480mins | Ready in:

Ingredients

- 2 lbs ground beef
- 2 (15 oz) cans tomato sauce
- 2 (14.5 oz) cans Hunt's petite diced tomatoes
- 2 (15 oz) cans pinto beans
- 2 (16 oz) cans of kidney beans (I like to get one can of dark red and one of light red. This is optional, since there's not much difference in taste... the variety of bean color just makes a prettier chili.)
- 2 (4.5 oz) cans Old El Paso chopped chilies
- 1 white onion (diced)
- 2 stalks celery (diced)
- 3 tablespoons chili powder
- 1 ½ teaspoons black pepper
- 2 teaspoons salt
- 2 teaspoons of cumin powder
- 1 cup water

Direction

- Brown the beef and drain off the fat.
- Combine the beef plus all the remaining ingredients into crock-pot. (Don't drain the liquid from the cans before mixing into chili.)
- Cover and cook on low, for several hours or overnight.

14. Crockpot Beef Chili Recipe

Serving: 6 | Prep: | Cook: 480mins | Ready in:

Ingredients

- 2-1/2 - pounds boneless beef chuck or round, cut into 1/2-inch pieces
- 2 - cans (15 ounces) black beans, rinsed and drained
- 1 - can (15 ounces) tomato sauce
- 1 - can (15 ounces) diced tomatoes
- 1 - can (14 ounces) beef broth
- 1 - medium onion, chopped
- 2 - teaspoon chili powder
- 1 - teaspoon salt
- 1 - teaspoon ground cumin
- 1/2 - teaspoon pepper
- 1 - cup prepared thick-and-chunky salsa (hot or mild - your choice)
- 1 jalapeño pepper, diced (optional)

Direction

- In 4 or 5-quart crockpot, add beef, black beans, tomato sauce, tomatoes, beef broth, onion, chili powder, salt, cumin and pepper (and jalapeño pepper, if using). Mix well. Cover and cook on HIGH 5-1/2 to 6 hours or on LOW 8 to 9 hours, or until beef is tender. (No stirring is necessary during cooking.) Just before serving, stir in salsa; cook 2 to 3 minutes or until heated through. Garnish with shredded cheddar cheese, diced onion, dairy sour cream, or sliced green onions, if desired

15. Crockpot Chili Beans Recipe

Serving: 10 | Prep: | Cook: 300mins | Ready in:

Ingredients

- 1 lb. of ground beef .1 onion. 1 green pepper. Can of tomatoe sauce. 1 Can of tomatoes. 1 teaspoon of chill powder. 1 teaspoon of onion powder. 1 teaspoon of garlic salt. Salt to tast. black pepper to tast. 1/2 cup of kectup. 1/4 cup of mustard. 3 strips of cooked bacon. One can of porkbean, one can of light kidney bean, one can of chili starter beans. And some time i use pinto beans.

Direction

- Cook bacon and drain off fat. Put onion and green pepper in pan and sauté. Then put in crock pot with the other ingredients cook until done. About 2 hours on high then 3 on low.

16. Crockpot Chili Recipe

Serving: 8 | Prep: | Cook: 180mins | Ready in:

Ingredients

- 2-1/2 to 3 lbs. ground beef
- 1 (15.5 oz.) can light red kidney beans, drained
- 1 (15.5 oz.) can dark red kidney beans, drained
- 1 (14.5 oz.) can diced tomatoes
- 1 (14.5 oz.) can stewed tomatoes
- 1/2 large yellow onion, diced
- 2 cloves garlic, finely minced
- 3/4 red pepper, coarsely chopped
- 1-3/4 Tbs. thyme, divided
- 1-3/4 tsp. red pepper flakes, divided
- 6 Tbs. chili powder, divided
- 1 Tbs. steak rub (Yes, steak!, recipe follows)
- 1 cup beef broth
- 5-1/2 pinches kosher salt, divided
- 2 to 2-1/2 Tbs. light brown sugar
- 1 Tbs. butter
- 1-1/2 Tbs. EVOO (extra virgin olive oil)
- steak RUB:
- **(From "Weber's Big Book of Grilling")**
- 2 tsp. black peppercorns
- 2 tsp. mustard seeds
- 2 tsp. paprika
- 1 tsp. granulated garlic
- 1 tsp. kosher salt
- 1 tsp. light brown sugar
- 1/4 tsp. cayenne pepper

Direction

- Preheat large skillet to medium low and heat EVOO and butter.
- Add garlic, sauté for about 1 minute, then add onions, 1/4 tsp. of the red pepper flake and 1 pinch kosher salt; sauté for about 5 minutes. Add chopped red pepper; sauté for another 5 minutes.
- Add 1/4 Tbs. chili powder and 1/4 Tbs. thyme; stir.
- Remove from heat and place in crock pot.
- Place skillet back on burner and increase heat to medium to medium-high, brown beef and drain fat.
- Season with salt, 1 tsp. red pepper, 4-3/4 Tbs. chili powder, 1 Tbs. thyme and all of the barbeque rub.
- Stir to combine and remove from heat.
- Add meat to crock pot with veggies, tomatoes and beans.
- Crank crock pot up to high, add remaining spices, brown sugar and beef broth; stir to combine.
- Put the lid on and walk away for about 2 to 3 hours.

17. Crockpot Chili Soup Recipe

Serving: 6 | Prep: | Cook: 240mins | Ready in:

Ingredients

- 1 pound lean ground beef, browned and drained
- 1 onion, chopped
- 2 (14 oz.) cans Rotel tomatoes
- 2 (14 oz.) cans ranch style beans
- 2 cans minestrone soup
- 1 Tablespoon chili

Direction

- Combine all ingredients in crockpot and cook for 4 hours.

18. Crockpot White Bean Chicken Chili Recipe

Serving: 12 | Prep: | Cook: 3mins | Ready in:

Ingredients

- 1 lb chicken, cut up into small chunks (I like to use boneless breasts for their "easy" and lower fat content)
- 1 cup chopped onion
- 1 can (or the equivalent) chicken broth
- 2 cloves of garlic, chopped finely
- 2 tsp cumin seed (ground will not withstand long cooking as well)
- 1/2 tsp dried oregano leaves
- 3 -15oz cans white beans (great northern or cannellini), drained and rinsed
- 1 or 2 chopped red, green or yellow bell peppers, or combination
- jalapeno chili peppers, fresh, jarred or canned, optional or 'to taste' (depending on how much heat you like!)

Direction

- In a 4 or 6 quart Crockpot combine the chicken, onions, chicken broth, garlic, cumin and oregano.
- Let cook awhile on low (approx. 3-5 hours, depending on your schedule)
- Add drained beans.
- I top with Monterey jack cheese and some homemade jalapeño cheese bread.

19. Crockpot White Chicken Chipolte Chili Recipe

Serving: 8 | Prep: | Cook: 300mins | Ready in:

Ingredients

- 2 cup cooked chicken
- 1 cup onions, Diced
- 1 medium pepper red bell pepper, Raw
- 1 pepper poblano pepper, Raw
- 2 tbsp garlic Minced
- 3 cup low sodium chicken broth
- 3 cup cannellini beans (canned)
- 1 1/2 cup great northern beans, canned
- 1 1/2 serving navy beans, canned, cooked
- 4 oz Diced Green Chiles
- 1 chipolte pepper in Adobe sauce + 1 tsp adobe sauce
- 1 1/2 cup stewed tomatoes, Original Recipe
- 1/4 tsp spices, cayenne pepper
- 1 tsp oregano, Ground
- 1 tsp salt

Direction

- The Chipotle Pepper gives the chili it's smoky, warm heat. You can find these canned in Adobe sauce in the Mexican section of the grocery store. Chop one up and make sure not to get any on your hands and then to your eyes. Very painful - yes I've done it.
- The beans in this recipe are canned. 1 typical 15oz can of beans measures into about 1.5 cups with its liquid. The stewed tomatoes are also a single can. Don't bother draining the beans - pour the liquid from the canned beans into the pot.
- CROCKPOT DIRECTIONS:
- Dice the onion and pepper. Mince the garlic. If using cooked chicken on the bone, remove the chicken from the bone. I used left-over, broiled chicken leg quarters. 2 cups from this chicken is 4 leg quarters.
- Process one cup chicken broth and 1 can cannellini beans in a blender or food processor until smooth.
- Put in all the remaining ingredients, stir, and cook on low for 4-6 hours.

20. Dads Crockpot Chili No Tomato Recipe

Serving: 8 | Prep: | Cook: 2mins | Ready in:

Ingredients

- 1/2 lb. ground beef
- 1/2 lb. pork sausage
- 1 large onion (diced)
- 1 large green pepper (diced)
- 2 Tbls. ground chili powder
- 1 cup water
- 2 beef bullion cubes
- 3 15oz. cans pinto beans (undrained)
- 3 15oz. cans great northern beans (undrained)
- 1 Level Tbls. cornstarch mixed in 1/2 cup water
- salt to taste

Direction

- In a large crockpot combine beans, bouillon cubes, water, onions, green peppers, chili powder.
- Fry ground beef and pork sausage and drain off fat.
- Add meat to bean mixture and cook on high for 6 hours
- Reduce heat to low for an additional 2 hours
- Turn off and let cool for about 15 minutes then stir in cornstarch and water mix
- Set aside to cool then refrigerate overnight.
- Can be eaten right away but I find its much better when reheated the next day.

21. Easy Chilli Recipe

Serving: 4 | Prep: | Cook: 4hours15mins | Ready in:

Ingredients

- 100 grams of lean ground beef
- One can of Heinz beans in water
- 1 medium onion (diced)
- 30g of green pepper
- 15g of mushroom
- 20g of celery
- 1/2 tsp of crushed red pepper
- 1/2 tsp of chilli powder
- 1/2 tsp of garlic (minced)
- 4 Sunset tomatoes (quartered)

Direction

- Fry lean ground beef and half the onion and garlic for about eight minutes, breaking into a crumble. You're just trying to break the beef apart. It will fully cook in the slow cooker.
- Place fried mixture into slow cooker with all other ingredients for 4 hours of low heat.

22. Easy Crock Pot Chili Cheese Dip Recipe

Serving: 12 | Prep: | Cook: 1mins | Ready in:

Ingredients

- 1 big box Velveeta cheese
- 1 can chili (I use chili Man Original)
- 1 can Rotel tomatoes

Direction

- Cut up cheese and dump it all in the crock pot! Wait about an hour, stir occasionally and enjoy!!! This is a quick easy summer favourite, and a great side to bbq!

23. Fire Nation Chili Recipe

Serving: 0 | Prep: | Cook: | Ready in:

Ingredients

- 2 cans dark kidney beans
- 2 cans light kidney beans
- 2 cans hot chili beans
- 2 cans tomato soup
- 1.5 lb ground beef (or for more kick use 1/2 beef and 1/2 hot sausage)
- 2 cans diced tomato with jalapeno

- 1 large onion diced
- 1 large green pepper diced
- 2 hot banana peppers diced
- 3 (or more) jalapenos diced (the more the hotter!!)
- 1/2 bottle Sriracha hot sauce (or as much as u feel is needed)
- 3 scoops of the hottest hot chili sause you can find
- crushed red pepper to taste
- *** include all seeds in chili***

Direction

- Brown beef
- Mix all ingredients together in slow cooker and cook on low to a boil.
- Be warned... you're going to be throwing flames like a fire bender after eating this tasty bowl of heat!!!
- ENJOY! =)

24. Homemade Beef Chili In The Crockpot Recipe

Serving: 8 | Prep: | Cook: 360mins | Ready in:

Ingredients

- 1 pound cooked ground beef
- 2 large cans crushed tomatoes
- 1/2 cup chili seasoning mix
- 6 cups cooked pinto beans
- 1 cup salsa
- 1 large white onion chopped
- Chili Seasoning Mix:
- 2/3 cup flour
- 3-1/2 cups minced dry onions
- 1-1/4 cup chili powder
- 3 tablespoons salt
- 2 tablespoons cumin
- 1/2 cup dried minced garlic
- 3 tablespoons red pepper flakes
- 3 tablespoons oregano

Direction

- Combine all mix ingredients and store in a cool dry place.
- Combine all ingredients in the crock pot and cook on low for 6 hours.

25. Homemade Pork Chili In The Crock Pot Recipe

Serving: 4 | Prep: | Cook: 360mins | Ready in:

Ingredients

- 1 pound cooked cubed pork
- 2 large cans crushed tomatoes
- 1/2 cup chili seasoning mix
- 6 cups cooked kidney beans
- 1 cup salsa
- 1 large white onion chopped
- Chili Seasoning Mix:
- 2/3 cup flour
- 3-1/2 cups minced dry onions
- 1-1/4 cup chili powder
- 3 tablespoons salt
- 2 tablespoons cumin
- 1/2 cup dried minced garlic
- 3 tablespoons red pepper flakes
- 3 tablespoons oregano

Direction

- Combine all mix ingredients and store in a cool dry place.
- Combine all ingredients in the crock pot and cook on low for 6 hours.

26. Jimmy Fallons Crock Pot Chili Recipe

Serving: 6 | Prep: | Cook: 300mins | Ready in:

Ingredients

- 2 tablespoons olive oil
- 3 1/2 pounds ground chuck beef, ground for chili
- coarse salt and freshly ground pepper
- 1 large white onion, chopped
- 3 cloves garlic, finely chopped
- 1/2 habanero chile, seeded and very finely chopped
- 1/4 cup chile powder
- 1 tablespoon dried oregano
- 1 1/2 teaspoons ground cumin
- 1/4 teaspoon cayenne pepper
- 2 (28-ounce) cans whole tomatoes, coarsely chopped with their juices
- 1/3 cup chopped fresh cilantro, plus more for serving
- 1 (12-ounce) bottle amber beer
- 2 (15-ounce) cans kidney beans, drained and rinsed
- tortilla chips, for serving
- Shredded cheddar cheese, for serving
- chopped tomatoes, for serving
- sour cream, for serving
- lime wedges, for serving

Direction

- In a large skillet, heat 1 tablespoon olive oil over medium-high heat. Working in batches if necessary, add beef and cook until no longer pink, about 3 minutes. Season with salt and pepper; drain in a colander, discarding fat, and set aside.
- Add remaining tablespoon olive oil to skillet and reduce heat to medium. Add onions, garlic, and habanero; season with salt. Cook until translucent, about 5 minutes.
- In a 6-quart Crock-Pot, combine beef, onion mixture, chile powder, oregano, cumin, and cayenne pepper; stir to combine. Add tomatoes, cilantro, and beer; cover and cook on high, stirring occasionally, for 5 hours.
- Add kidney beans and season with salt and pepper. Continue to cook, uncovered, until thickened, about 30 minutes. Garnish with cilantro and serve with desired toppings.

27. Kate's Google Chili Recipe

Serving: 0 | Prep: | Cook: 3hours | Ready in:

Ingredients

- 2 1/2 lb. lean chuck, ground
- 1 lb. lean pork, ground
- 4 garlic cloves, finely chopped
- 1 cup finely chopped onion
- 8 oz. hunt's tomato sauce
- 1 cup water
- 1 can beer (12 oz.) (I used Sam Adams)
- 3 Tablespoons chili powder (I used Bloemer's)
- 2 Tablespoons instant beef bouillon (or 6 cubes)
- 2 Tablespoons cumin, ground
- 2 teaspoons paprika
- 2 teaspoons oregano leaves
- 2 teaspoons sugar
- 1/2 teaspoon coriander, ground
- 1 teaspoon unsweetened cocoa (I had to use Hershey's, I'd say get something better if you can)
- 1/2 teaspoon Louisiana hot sauce
- 1 teaspoon cornmeal
- 1 teaspoon flour
- 1 teaspoon warm water
- 1/2 c tequila
- 2 ears fresh corn (optional)
- 1 1/2 chopped jalapeno (optional)
- juice of 1 lime
- 2 tbsp chipotle chili powder
- 1 can black beans or kidney beans

Direction

- Directions:
- 1. In a large saucepan brown 1 1/4 pounds of the ground meat (the beef and the pork), drain the fat.

- 2. Remove meat (the beef and the pork). Brown the rest of the ground meat, drain all but 2 tablespoons of the fat.
- 3. Add the garlic and onion, cook and stir until tender.
- 4. Add the other half of the meat and the tomato sauce, water, beer, chili powder, bouillon, cumin, paprika, oregano, sugar, coriander, cocoa, and hot sauce. Mix well.
- 5. Bring to a boil then reduce heat and simmer, covered, for 2 hours.
- 6. In a small bowl, stir together the cornmeal and flour, then add the warm water and mix well.
- 7. Stir into chili and cook, covered, for an additional 20 minutes.
- Special Additions I make:
- Salt and Pepper in the beef while browning it, to taste
- 2 ears fresh white corn, cut off the cob
- Juice of 1 lime
- 1 1/2 fresh Jalapenos, chopped fine. Add 1 before cooking it down, and 1/2 in your second spice dump
- I reduced the chili powder by 1 Tbsp., and replaced it with 1 Tbsp. chipotle chili powder
- The oregano that I used was fresh & organic
- I also used fresh garlic, 5 large cloves.
- I added tequila, Jose Cuervo gold. 1/2 cup tequila, add 1/4 cup at first then 1/4 cup at the end before re-heating and serving
- Instead of just 8 oz. tomato sauce, also added 8oz diced tomatoes with chilies.
- Beef Bouillon was bouillon paste, 8 tsp. use the good stuff.
- 1 can of kidney beans, liquid drained off
- Added extra hot sauce, 1 Tbsp. Frank's
- Extra beer, 1/2 cup or to taste
- 2nd spice dump I made at the end before re-heating:
- 1 tbsp. Bloemer's chili powder, 1Tbsp Chipotle chili powder, 1 tsp Paprika, 1/4 tsp coriander, 1 Tbsp. cumin, 2 tsp oregano, 1Tbsp Frank's Louisiana hot sauce, ½ tsp cocoa powder , ½ Jalapeno pepper, diced & 1 more tsp sugar, or to taste
- I cooked it on low in a crock pot for 6 hours. Not sure it needs to cook that long though.
- I also got a tip from a chef I know, which is to toast the spices. Put your dry spices in a dry sauté pan and heat them up on high heat. When you see the first whiff of smoke, remove them from the heat, then add them to the chili. I guess this does not mean any of the herbs, just the chili powder or any pepper you use. I did not try this, but it is supposed to bring out all of the flavor.

28. My Chili Ctme Recipe

Serving: 0 | Prep: | Cook: 11hours | Ready in:

Ingredients

- 2 1/2 to 3 lbs   ground beef
- 1 1/2 lb   ground pork
- 1   lb   regular or hot chorizo sausage or sweet or hot Italian sausage
- 1   large yellow onion, diced
- 2 T   large cloves garlic, minced or minced garlic from jar
- 1 (14oz/cn) mushrooms, sliced or fresh shrooms sliced
- 1 lg/cn or 3 sm/cns Kuner's chili beans in hot sauce, undrained
- 3 (16oz/cns) Kuner's Mexican Style tomatoes with herbs or rotel   diced tomatoes & green chilies, undrained
- 3 (4oz/cns)   diced green chilies or small container Buenos diced green chilies
- 2 T   ground cumin
- 4 to 6 T   Chimayo red chili powder or equivalent
- 1 tsp   chili Pequin (optional (hot)
- 1 to 2 tsp   Mexican oregano, measured after slightly crushed
- salt & fresh ground black pepper to taste

Direction

- Using a 4 qtr. slow-cooker or larger, add tomatoes, chili beans, green chilies, chili powder, chili Pequin (if using), oregano, and salt/pepper. Stir well and set heat to HIGH for first hour.
- In a large skillet brown the beef, pork and sausage until mostly done. Drain fat reserving about 2 tablespoons in skillet. Add meat to slow-cooker and mix well.
- Add the onions, garlic and mushrooms to skillet and sauté until onions turn translucent, about 8 to 10 minutes. Stir frequently. Add to slow-cooker, mix well and set to LOW, cover and cook for 6 to 8 hours, stirring occasionally.
- Highly recommend refrigerating overnight and reheating the next day for maximum flavor.
- Can serve with cornbread, bowls of shredded Cheddar cheese, crushed saltines, sliced/diced green onions, sour cream and a good Mexican beer, or Chianti for beverage.

29. My Chili Valentine Recipe

Serving: 0 | Prep: | Cook: 8hours15mins | Ready in:

Ingredients

- 1.5 lbs ground beef (chuck)
- 1 tsp chili powder
- 1 tsp paprika
- 1 tsp garlic powder
- 1 tsp onion powder
- 1/4 tsp cayenne pepper (more or less to taste)
- 1 tsp seasoning salt (Lawry's)
- 1 cup chopped onion
- 2 cloves garlic, minced
- 1 14.5 oz. can diced tomatoes, with liquid
- 1 8 oz.can tomato sauce
- 2 7 oz. cans diced mild green chilies, drained
- 1 15 oz. can pink beans, drained and rinsed
- 1 15 oz. can red kidney beans, drained and rinsed
- 1 cup beef stock
- 1/4 cup A1 steak sauce
- 2 fresh bay leaves
- 2 tbsp brown sugar
- 1 tsp chili powder
- 1 tsp paprika
- 1 tsp garlic powder
- 1 tsp onion powder
- 1/4 cayenne pepper (more or less to taste)
- 1 tsp seasoning salt (Lawry's)

Direction

- Heat 1/4 cup water in a skillet over medium heat. Brown beef and season with following 6 ingredients. Drain and place in crock pot.
- Add onion, garlic, tomatoes, tomato sauce, chilies, beans, A1, beef stock and bay leaves. Add remaining seasoning. Mix all together.
- Cook on low for 8 hours.

30. New And Improved Crock Pot Pork Chili Verde Recipe

Serving: 10 | Prep: | Cook: 480mins | Ready in:

Ingredients

- 3 lbs pork shoulder
- 28 oz can green tomatillos
- 7 oz can of diced green chili's
- 10 oz can of diced red tomatoes
- 1 tbls cumin
- pinch of salt
- pinch of pepper
- 2 chopped cloves of garlic
- 1 medium onion
- 5 anaheim chiles
- 2 jalapeno peppers
- 1/2 bottle of mexican beer(i use Pacifico or Tecate)

Direction

- Clean and de-seed the Anaheim and jalapeno chiles. Dry good, rub with a little oil and cook

under broiler turning ever few minutes. Chiles will be a little black but not entirely when done. Put Chiles into a Ziploc bag for about 10 minutes. Now easily remove the skin and add to crock pot.
- Chop the garlic and dice and brown the onion in a skillet with a little oil. Put into crock pot.
- Cut the pork into cubes. Add to skillet and cook until just brown on sides. Put into crock pot.
- Deglaze pan with beer and pour into crock pot.
- Chop tomatillos in food processor or blender.
- Pour tomatillos, green chilies, cumin, salt and pepper into crock pot.
- Stir everything together.
- Cook on High for 1 hour.
- Switch to Low and cook for another 7 hours.
- (Crock pot liner works great)
- Serve with refried beans and rice. Makes excellent burritos!

31. Rustic Chili Recipe

Serving: 8 | Prep: | Cook: 8hours | Ready in:

Ingredients

- 2lbs beef or venison roast or steaks, cubed(you can use a lesser cut of meat here, no problem)
- about 1 1/2 cups cooked black beans
- about 1 1/2 cups cooked black eyes peas
- about 2 cups crushed tomatoes
- about 1 cup diced tomatoes
- about 6oz tomato paste
- 1 large onion, chopped
- 6 cloves garlic, minced
- 1T dried Mexican oregano(or sub a couple T fresh)
- 2t ground cumin
- 2t ground coriander
- 1T chili powder
- 1/2-2t ground cayenne
- 1/2-1T ancho, pasilla or chipotle chili powder
- 1-4 fresh jalapenos or similar hot pepper, chopped
- 1-2 bell peppers, chopped
- about 1/4 cup red wine or balsamic vinegar
- 16oz bottle of dark beer
- couple dashes of liquid smoke
- kosher or sea salt and fresh ground pepper
- sour cream, chopped green onions, shredded cheese to serve

Direction

- Combine all ingredients in slow cooker and cook on low for at least 8 hours, up to 12 or so.
- Stir occasionally after the first hours, and remove lid an hour or so prior to serving, if desired, to thicken.

32. Slo Cooker Chili Recipe

Serving: 8 | Prep: | Cook: 8hours | Ready in:

Ingredients

- cooking spray
- 1 pound ground beef
- 1/2 pound ground pork
- 3 cups chopped onion
- 1 3/4 cups chopped green bell pepper
- 3 garlic cloves, minced
- 3 tablespoons tomato paste
- 3 tablespoons chili powder
- 1 tablespoon ground cumin
- 2 teaspoons dried oregano
- 3/4 teaspoon freshly ground black pepper
- 6 tomatillos, quartered
- 2 bay leaves
- 2 (14 1/2-ounce) cans plum tomatoes, undrained and chopped
- 1 (15-ounce) can no-salt-added pinto beans, drained
- 1 (7 3/4-ounce) can Mexican hot-style tomato sauce (such as El Paso)
- 1 smoked ham hock (about 8 oz)
- 1 1/2 tablespoons sugar

- 1/2 cup finely chopped cilantro
- 1/2 cup finely chopped green onions
- 1/2 cup (2 ounces) shredded cheese
- 8 lime wedges

Direction

- 1. Heat a large nonstick skillet over medium-high heat. Coat pan with cooking spray. Add ground pork to pan; cook 5 minutes or until browned, stirring to slightly crumble. Drain well. Brown ground beef as well. Transfer to an electric slow cooker.
- 2. Recoat pan with cooking spray. Add onion and bell pepper; sauté 8 minutes, stirring frequently. Add garlic; sauté 1 minute. Add tomato paste; cook 1 minute, stirring constantly. Transfer onion mixture to slow cooker. Add chili powder, and next 9 ingredients (through ham hock) to slow cooker. Cover and cook on Low 8 hours or until meat is tender. Remove bay leaves and ham hock; discard. Stir in sugar. Ladle about 1 1/3 cups chili into each of 8 bowls; top each serving with 1 tablespoon cilantro, 1 tablespoon green onions, and 1 tablespoon cheese. Serve each serving with 1 wedge of lime.

33. Slow Cooker Beef Chili Recipe

Serving: 6 | Prep: | Cook: 480mins | Ready in:

Ingredients

- 2 lbs. of lean beef cubes cut into bite size
- 1 green pepper diced
- 1 red pepper diced
- 1 vidalia onion sliced thin
- 1 (14 oz) can of dark red kidney beans drained and rinsed
- 1 (14 oz) can of fire roasted tomatoes (I like Hunts)
- 1 (28oz) can of crushed tomatoes
- 1 c. of low sodium beef broth (or stock if you like)
- 2 pks. of chili seasoning (I like McCormick)
- 1 tblspn of olive oil

Direction

- Sautee' the peppers and onion in olive oil for about 5-7 minutes.
- Add with all other ingredients into a slow cooker and mix thoroughly. Cook for 8-10 hours on low.
- Serve with a dollop of sour cream, shredded cheese, and tortilla chips!
- Enjoy!

34. Slow Cooker Chicken Chili Recipe

Serving: 6 | Prep: | Cook: 300mins | Ready in:

Ingredients

- 10 3/4 ounces condensed cream of chicken soup
- 10 3/4 ounces Garden Fresh Gourmet Jack's Special Medium salsa
- 10 3/4 ounces low sodium chicken broth
- 1 onion, chopped
- 1 garlic clove, pressed
- 4.5 ounce can green chilies, chopped
- 1 1/4 ounce chili-O seasoning (or taco seasoning)
- 1 teaspoon cumin
- 15.5 ounces black beans, drained and rinsed
- 15.5 ounces great northern beans, drained and rinsed
- 15.5 ounces pinto beans, drained and rinsed
- 6 boneless, skinless chicken breasts (no need to thaw)
- 6 ounce package Mexican rice
- 1 Tablespoon lime juice
- ¼ cup Tablespoons fresh cilantro, chopped
- 3 cups colby cheese, shredded

Direction

- In slow cooker, stir together cream of chicken soup, salsa, and chicken broth until smooth. Stir onion, garlic, chilies, Chili-O, and cumin until well mixed. Gently stir in beans. Place chicken in crock pot and use a spoon to push to the bottom of the slow cooker.
- Cover and cook on low for 5 hours.
- Remove chicken and cut into bite size chunks. Return chicken to slow cooker.
- Prepare rice according to package directions.
- Just before serving, stir in prepared rice, lime juice, cilantro, and 1 cup of shredded cheese.
- Serve with remaining 2 cups of cheese sprinkled on top.

35. Slow Cooker Chili Beef Stew Recipe

Serving: 6 | Prep: | Cook: 27mins | Ready in:

Ingredients

- 1 1/2 lb beef stew meat
- 4 medium potatoes, cut into 1-inch pieces
- 1 medium onion, coarsely chopped (3/4 cup)
- 3 cans (14.5 oz each) diced tomatoes with zesty mild green chilies, undrained
- 1 3/4 cups beef flavored broth (from 32-oz carton)
- 1 tablespoon chili powder
- 2 teaspoons ground cumin
- 1 teaspoon garlic salt
- 1/8 teaspoon pepper

Direction

- In 3 1/2- to 4-quart slow cooker, mix all ingredients.
- Cover; cook on Low heat setting 9 to 10 hours.

36. Slow Cooker Chili Recipe

Serving: 12 | Prep: | Cook: 360mins | Ready in:

Ingredients

- 1 1/2 pound ground chuck
- 1 pound hot pork sausage
- 2 garlic cloves-minced
- 1 14 1/2oz can tomatoes-whole,crushed,stewed,or diced
- 1 8oz can tomato sauce
- 1 6oz can tomato paste
- 1 large onion-chopped
- 1 medium bell pepper-chopped
- 2 15oz cans kidney beans-drained
- 1/4 cup brown sugar-light or dark
- 1 tablespoon chili powder
- 1 teaspoon salt
- 1 teaspoon black pepper
- 1 teaspoon crushed red pepper
- 1 teaspoon cayenne pepper.

Direction

- Brown ground chuck and sausage in large skillet.
- Drain and transfer to slow cooker/crock pot (4 quart or larger).
- Add remaining ingredients and mix well.
- Cover and cook on low for 8-10 hours or high for 4-6 hours.
- If chili becomes too thick, add a little water.
- Can be served with corn bread and topped with sour cream, chopped raw onion, cheddar cheese, or whatever you like.

37. Slow Cooker Mexican Pork Chili Recipe

Serving: 10 | Prep: | Cook: 390mins | Ready in:

Ingredients

- 2-3 lb pork roast

- 4 tomatillos- diced
- 5 cloves garlic-minced
- 3 tablespoon red cooking wine
- 1 tablespoon vinegar
- 1 teaspoon chili ancho powder
- 2 bay leaves
- 1/2 teaspoon ground cumin
- 1/4 teaspoon Mexican oregano
- 2 teaspoons dried cilantro
- 1/2 teaspoon cracked pepper
- 3 tablespoon tomato paste
- 3 chipotle chilies in adobo w/ sauce-minced
- 2 cups water
- 2 tablespoons chicken bouillon
- 1 white onion minced
- 2- 15oz cans black beans, rinsed and drained
- 1- 15oz can red beans, rinsed and drained
- Toppings:
- Green onions- chopped
- crumbles queso freso
- limes
- tortilla chips

Direction

- Place pork roast in slow cooker, add all dry ingredients except chicken bouillon over pork roast.
- Then add all remaining ingredient to crock pot, except beans! Mix water and chicken bouillon together, then add to crock pot. Cook on high for about 5 hours.
- After 5 hours remove lid and shred pork and remove bone if you used bone in roast, then add beans and mix together. Cover and let cook another 1-1/2 hours.
- Serve in bowls and top with crumbled queso fresco, green onions, limes and tortilla chips.

38. Slow Cooker Pork Butt Green Chili Recipe

Serving: 6 | Prep: | Cook: 5mins | Ready in:

Ingredients

- 3 to 4 pounds bone-in pork butt, trimmed and cut into large chunks, or 1 1/2 pounds boneless pork butt
- 1 (27-ounce) can (or 7 4-ounce cans) chopped mild green chiles
- 1 head garlic, cloves peeled and left whole
- 3 canned chipotle chiles, or to taste
- 2 teaspoons ground cumin
- 2 tablespoons all-purpose flour, mixed with 2 cups cold water
- salt and pepper
- flour tortillas or rice for serving
- sour cream, optional

Direction

- Place the pork, green chiles, garlic, chipotles, ground cumin and flour-water mixture in a slow cooker and set to desired temperature. Cover pot and cook until pork is tender enough to pierce easily with a fork (at least 5 hours if set on high).
- Remove meat from pot and shred to desired thickness.
- With a wooden spoon mash garlic and chiles and spoon over pork. Season to taste with salt and pepper.
- Roll in tortillas, or serve over rice, and serve with sour cream if desired.

39. Slow Cooker Pumpkin Chili Recipe

Serving: 8 | Prep: | Cook: 5hours | Ready in:

Ingredients

- 2 pounds ground beef
- 2 cans pumpkin puree
- 2 cans diced tomatoes
- 1 onion, diced
- 1 can kidney beans, drained
- 2 tsp. pumpkin pie spice

- 1/2 tsp. red pepper
- 1 tsp. chili powder
- 1 tsp. of black pepper if desired

Direction

- Brown meat lightly in skillet. Add onions and cook until just tender.
- Put remaining ingredients in slow cooker and fold in meat mixture.
- Cook on high for 1 hour, then turn to low for 5 hours.

40. Slow Cooker White Bean And Chicken Chili Recipe

Serving: 8 | Prep: | Cook: 360mins | Ready in:

Ingredients

- 2 (15 oz.) cans white beans, rinsed and drained
- 4 c. low-sodium chicken broth
- 1 TBSP. vegetable oil
- 2 whole bone-in chicken breasts (3 lb.)
- salt and pepper
- 2 onions, chopped
- 4 cloves garlic, chopped
- 2 (4 oz.) cans roasted, chopped green chilies
- 1 TBSP. ground cumin

Direction

- Warm oil in skillet over medium-high heat. Sprinkle chicken with salt and pepper. Place chicken skin side down in skillet; cook until brown, about 4 minutes. Turn and cook for 2 minutes more. Transfer to a plate; remove and discard skin. Drain all but 2 Tbsp. fat from skillet. Add onions and garlic; cook until softened, 5 minutes. Add onion mixture, chilies, beans, broth, and cumin to slow cooker. Stir; add chicken breasts.
- Cook on low for 6 hours, stirring twice. Remove 1 cup beans plus 1/2 cup liquid from slow cooker. Puree in a blender; return to slow cooker. Remove chicken, shred it and return to slow cooker. Spoon into individual bowls and serve.
- I used 4 small boneless, skinless chicken breasts - it's what I had in the freezer, and this chili turned out delicious all the same!

41. Slow Cooker Black Bean Chili Recipe

Serving: 8 | Prep: | Cook: 22mins | Ready in:

Ingredients

- black beans go into the slow cooker with an army of flavorful ingredients. So why is the result so often a dull, muddied mess? Here's what we discovered:
- Test Kitchen Discoveries
- To build assertive flavor, start by sautéing chopped onion, bell pepper, garlic, and jalapeños in a Dutch oven; beginning the sauté with bacon fat, rather than the usual oil, also helps amplify the meaty richness of the chili.
- The test kitchen likes to sauté spices to intensify their flavor. When the vegetables are tender, add 1/4 cup of chili powder, plus cumin and oregano, and let the spices bloom in the hot pan.
- While ham hocks traditionally add flavor and a few shreds of meat to the chili, we wanted enough meat to chew on. We opted for the salty richness a small smoked ham lent to the chili as it cooked; removing the ham at the end of cooking and chopping it provided plenty of meat.
- dried beans added to the slow cooker at the outset were still too hard by the time the chili was done. To speed up the cooking, we simmer the beans in the Dutch oven for 15 minutes before transferring the contents to the slow cooker.

- For the right combination of creamy whole beans and a thick, rich chili, we mashed a can of black beans into the base of slow-cooked dried black beans.

Direction

- We prefer the sweetness of red bell peppers here, but any bell pepper will work. Small boneless hams are available in the meat case at most supermarkets. The aluminum foil in step 2 helps keep all the beans under the surface of the liquid, where they cook evenly. We like to serve this chili with sour cream, shredded Monterey Jack cheese, and fresh cilantro.
- 8 slices bacon, chopped
- 2 onions, chopped fine
- 2 red bell peppers, seeded and chopped (see note)
- 2 jalapeño chiles, seeded and chopped fine
- 1/4 cup chili powder
- 2 tablespoons ground cumin
- 2 tablespoons dried oregano
- 5 garlic cloves, minced
- 6 cups water
- 4 cups low-sodium chicken broth
- Salt
- 1 1/2 pounds dried black beans, rinsed and picked over
- 1 boneless ham (1 to 1 1/2 pounds) (see note)
- 1 (28-ounce) can diced tomatoes
- 1 (15.5-ounce) can black beans, drained and rinsed
- 3 tablespoons fresh lime juice from 2 limes
- 1. Cook bacon in Dutch oven over medium heat until crisp, about 8 minutes. Transfer bacon to paper towel-lined plate. Cook onions, peppers, and jalapeños in bacon fat until softened, about 8 minutes. Transfer half of sautéed vegetables to medium bowl, wrap with plastic, and reserve in refrigerator. Add chili powder, cumin, and oregano to pot with remaining vegetables and cook until deeply fragrant, about 2 minutes. Add garlic and cook until fragrant, about 30 seconds. Stir in water, broth, 2 teaspoons salt, dried beans, ham, and crisp bacon. Bring to boil and let simmer 15 minutes.
- 2. Transfer bean mixture to slow cooker and arrange piece of aluminum foil on surface of liquid. Cover and cook on low until beans are tender, 7 to 9 hours (or cook on high 4 to 6 hours).
- 3. Remove lid, discard foil, and transfer ham to cutting board. Stir tomatoes into slow cooker, cover, and cook on high until tomatoes soften, about 20 minutes. Meanwhile, transfer canned beans to bowl and mash with potato masher until rough paste forms. Chop (or shred) ham into bite-sized pieces. Stir mashed beans, ham, lime juice, and refrigerated vegetables into slow cooker. Cook, covered, until heated through, about 5 minutes. Season with salt. Serve.

42. Slow Cooker Chili Recipe

Serving: 6 | Prep: | Cook: 3mins | Ready in:

Ingredients

- 1 1/2 lbs ground beef
- 2 (15 oz) cans red kindey beans or small red beans, rinsed and drained
- 2 (14.5 oz) Cans Mexican-style stewed tomatoes, undrained (I used Ro-tel Mild diced tomatoes)
- 1 (16 oz) jar salsa (I used Pace Mild chunky salsa)
- 3/4 cup chopped onion (1 large)
- 3/4 cup chopped green sweet pepper (1 medium)
- 1 clove garlic, minced
- Desired toppers, such as sliced green onions, corn chips, chopped tomatoes, and/or shredded cheddar cheese

Direction

- 1. In a large skillet, brown ground beef, over medium heat. Drain off fat. Transfer meat to

a 4- or 5-quart slow cooker. Add beans, tomatoes, salsa, onion, sweet pepper, and garlic to beef in slow cooker; stir to combine.
- 2. Cover and cook on low-heat setting for 10 to 12 hours or on high-heat setting for 5 to 6 hours. Serve chili with desired toppings.

43. Spicy Pork Green Chili Crock Pot Recipe

Serving: 6 | Prep: | Cook: 480mins | Ready in:

Ingredients

- 6 cups water
- 1 chopped onion
- 1 large can of diced green chilis (27oz)
- 1 tbsp diced jalepenos
- 1 tbsp garlic paste
- 1 tbsp paprika
- 1/2 cup sugar *(more or less as desired)
- 1.5 lbs cubed pork roast
- 1 cup stewed tomatoes
- 1 can (15 oz) great northern beans
- 1 cup sliced mushrooms *(optional)
- 1/2 cup chopped celery *(optional)
- 1 cup shredded cheddar
- sour cream *(optional)
- Tortill chips or flour tortillas

Direction

- Add all ingredients (except cheese, sour cream & chips) to CROCK POT
- Set on low for 8 hours
- Serve with cheese and sour cream.
- Serve over tortilla chips or soup style with ripped tortillas to dunk

44. Stupid Easy Crock Pot Chili Recipe

Serving: 8 | Prep: | Cook: 240mins | Ready in:

Ingredients

- 2 lbs. lean ground beef, cooked and drained
- 1 tbsp onion powder
- 2 tsp minced garlic
- 1 16-oz jar picante sauce (mild, medium or hot)
- 2 14-1/2 oz cans diced tomatoes, undrained
- 1 1.25 oz packet taco seasoning (mild, medium or hot)
- 2 15 oz cans chili beans in sauce
- 1 15.5 oz can dark red kidney beans, undrained
- 1 15 oz can black beans, undrained
- 3 tbsp chili powder
- 2 tbsp ground cumin
- 1/2 tsp salt (optional)
- 1 tsp black pepper
- 1 tsp oregano
- ½ to 2 tsp red pepper flakes

Direction

- Mix all ingredients in Crock Pot. Cover; cook on HIGH for 3 to 4 hours.
- Note: To make on stovetop, mix all ingredients in a big soup pot; cover and simmer for about an hour or so.

45. Tailgate Slow Cooker Chili Recipe

Serving: 18 | Prep: | Cook: 480mins | Ready in:

Ingredients

- 1 lb ground sirlion
- 1 lb pork tenderlion
- 1lb beef chuck roast
- 3/4 lb hot italian sausage

- 24 oz. tomato sauce chunky style
- 6 cups water (or half beer and half water)
- 4 beef buoillon cubes
- 1 1/2 cups onion (large dice)
- 2 chipotile peppers (more if you like more heat)
- 4 tbsps chili powder
- salt and pepper to taste
- 2 cups peppers (larger dice)optional
- 1 14oz can kidney beans

Direction

- Combine all ingredients in slow cooker except for kidney beans...cook for 6-8 hours until meat is falling apart.
- Add beans and cook 20-30 mins longer - check for spice - add as needed.
- If you want to do this stove top it's easily done - just cut your meats into bite size pieces and brown with onions and peppers. Add the rest of the ingredients and cook over low heat for 4 hrs. stirring frequently.

46. Turkey Chili For The Crock Pot Recipe

Serving: 10 | Prep: | Cook: 240mins | Ready in:

Ingredients

- 2 pounds ground turkey
- 1 cup chopped onion
- 4 large cloves of garlic, chopped
- 1/2 cup diced sweet bell pepper
- 1/2 cup diced pasilla pepper
- 1 cup low salt chicken broth
- 1 teaspoon dried oregano
- 1/2 teaspoon chili powder or to desired taste
- 1/2 teaspoon chile de arbol or to desired taste
- 2 ~ large cans red kidney beans, 1 drained and 1 undrained

Direction

- In a large skillet brown the ground turkey with the onions, garlic and peppers, drain. Add all of the ingredients to the crock pot, stir and cover. Cook on low 4 ~ 6 hours, serve with warm buttered cornbread.
- (For easier cleanup spray the crock pot with a nonstick spray before adding all of the ingredients.)

47. Vegan Slow Cooker Chili Recipe

Serving: 8 | Prep: | Cook: 420mins | Ready in:

Ingredients

- 1 bag Morningstar Farms® Meal Starters™ Grillers™ Recipe Crumbles™
- 1 14oz mild can diced tomatoes undrained and pureed
- 1 12oz can tomato paste
- 8-12oz water (use tomato paste can)
- 1 (15 ounce) can kidney beans, drained and rinsed
- 1 (15 ounce) can black beans, drained and rinsed
- Frozen diced bell peppers and onion. Or 1 bell pepper and 1/2-1 fresh onion diced.
- 2 cloves garlic
- sprinkling dried basil
- sprinkling of salt
- sprinkling of black pepper
- Little less then 2 Tablespoons packed organic brown sugar
- 1 teaspoon paprika
- 1-2 teaspoons ground chipotle pepper
- 1 teaspoon garlic powder
- 2 teaspoons ground cumin

Direction

- Combine everything in the slow cooker.
- Let sit overnight if you have time.
- Cook on low for 6 to 10 hours. Or on high for 3.5.

- Serve over fries, hash browns, or with corn chips or bread.

48. Vegetarian Crockpot Chili Recipe

Serving: 6 | Prep: | Cook: 24mins | Ready in:

Ingredients

- 1 (11 ounce) can condensed black bean soup
- 1 (15 ounce) can kidney beans, drained and rinsed
- 1 (15 ounce) can garbanzo beans, drained and rinsed
- 1 (16 ounce) can vegetarian baked beans
- 1 (14.5 ounce) can chopped tomatoes in puree
- 1 (15 ounce) can whole kernel corn, drained
- 1 onion, chopped
- 1 green bell pepper, chopped
- 2 stalks celery, chopped
- 2 cloves garlic, chopped
- 1 Tbs chili powder
- 1 Tbs dried parsley
- 1 Tbs dried oregano
- 1 Tbs dried basil

Direction

- In a crockpot, combine black bean soup, kidney beans, garbanzo beans, baked beans, tomatoes, corn, onion, bell pepper and celery.
- Season with garlic, chili powder, parsley, oregano and basil.
- Cook 4 hours on high or 8 hours on low

49. Vegetarian Crock Pot Chili Recipe

Serving: 8 | Prep: | Cook: 6mins | Ready in:

Ingredients

- 5 stalks celery, chopped
- 3-4 assorted peppers, chopped and deseeded (most any small to medium size pepper will do. Some supermarkets sell them in variety packs.) You can also use bell pepper here if you like it, or even a jalapeno
- 1 large onion, chopped
- 2 medium zucchini squash, chopped
- 2 cans of diced tomatoes, chili-ready if available
- 1 large can chili beans
- 1 med. can niblet corn
- 3 tbs. sherry cooking wine
- 1 package dry tortellini, 4 or 5 cheese kind
- 2 tbs. cumin
- 2 tbs. chili powder
- 3/4 cup water

Direction

- In crock pot, combine tomatoes and beans.
- In skillet, sauté in olive oil the vegetables until crisp-tender. Add to vegetable mixture 1 tbs. of the cumin and the chili powder. Salt and pepper to taste. Toward end of cooking, add sherry and deglaze pan.
- Add vegetable mixture to tomatoes and beans in crock pot.
- Add corn to crock pot
- Add remaining spices, but monitor as you cook for you might want more.
- Cook for 5 hours on high, stirring occasionally.
- Add 3/4 cup of water and the tortellini
- Continue to cook until tortellini have reached al dente stage.

50. Very Old Meatloaf Recipe

Serving: 6 | Prep: | Cook: 181mins | Ready in:

Ingredients

- 2 pounds ground beef
- 2 tablespoons water
- 1 tablespoon milk

- 1 cup bread crumbs
- 1 onion, diced
- 1 carrot, diced
- 1 small Granny Smith apple, diced
- 1 egg

Direction

- Preheat the oven to 375 degrees F (190 degrees C).
- Mix ground beef with water and milk in a large bowl using your hands until beef is evenly moistened.
- Mix bread crumbs, onion, carrot, apple, and egg into the beef mixture until evenly integrated.
- Form the beef mixture into a loaf.
- Transfer the meatloaf to a deep baking dish; tent with a sheet of aluminum foil.
- Bake in preheated oven for 1 hour; remove foil tent and bake until no longer pink the center, about 30 minutes more.
- Nutrition Facts
- Per Serving:
- 289.2 calories; protein 22.2g 44% DV; carbohydrates 15g 5% DV; fat 15.1g 23% DV; cholesterol 94.4mg 32% DV; sodium 181.3mg 7% DV.

Index

B
Bacon 3,4
Beans 3,9
Beef 3,9,13,15,18,19
Black pepper 7

C
Cheddar 16
Cheese 3,4,12
Chicken 3,8,11,18,21
Chilli 3,12
Chipotle 3,5,11,15
Coriander 7
Crumble 24
Cumin 7

D
Dijon mustard 4

G
Garlic 7

H
Hominy 3,8

J
Jus 9,19

M
Meat 3,25
Mince 11
Mushroom 3,4

N
Nut 26

O
Onion 7

P
Paprika 7,15
Pepper 7,11,15
Pork 3,7,13,16,19,20,23
Pumpkin 3,20

S
Salt 9,15,22,25
Seasoning 13
Soup 3,10
Stew 3,19
Sugar 3,4

T
Tea 7
Tomato 3,11
Turkey 3,24

V
Vegan 3,24
Vegetarian 3,25

W
White sugar 5

Conclusion

Thank you again for downloading this book!

I hope you enjoyed reading about my book!

If you enjoyed this book, please take the time to share your thoughts and post a review on Amazon. It'd be greatly appreciated!

Write me an honest review about the book – I truly value your opinion and thoughts and I will incorporate them into my next book, which is already underway.

Thank you!

If you have any questions, **feel free to contact at:** author@limerecipes.com

Carol Miller

limerecipes.com

Made in United States
Orlando, FL
18 November 2024